GREAT WESTERN
BRANCH LINE GALLERY

Front cover: *A Kingsbridge branch train pauses at Avonwick on its way to Brent in Devon (see also page 109). Since closure of the line in 1963, the station buildings have been sympathetically converted for residential use and the platform retained.* (Great Western Trust)

Rear cover: *This is a Fairford-bound train at Lechlade in Oxfordshire (see also pages 12-13 & 103). The fireman appears to be washing out his billycan with the hose.* (Great Western Trust)

GREAT WESTERN
BRANCH LINE GALLERY

KEVIN McCORMACK

PEN & SWORD
TRANSPORT
AN IMPRINT OF PEN & SWORD BOOKS LTD.
YORKSHIRE – PHILADELPHIA

First published in Great Britain in 2023 by
Pen and Sword Transport
An imprint of
Pen & Sword Books Ltd.
Yorkshire - Philadelphia

Copyright © Kevin McCormack, 2023

ISBN 978 1 39909 871 7

The right of Kevin McCormack to be identified as author of this work has been asserted by him in accordance with the Copyright, Designs and Patents Act 1988.

A CIP catalogue record for this book is available from the British Library.

All rights reserved. No part of this book may be reproduced or transmitted in any form or by any means, electronic or mechanical including photocopying, recording or by any information storage and retrieval system, without permission from the Publisher in writing.

Typeset in 11/13.5 pt Times New Roman by SJmagic DESIGN SERVICES, India.
Printed and bound in India by Replika Press Pvt. Ltd.

Pen & Sword Books Ltd incorporates the imprints of Pen & Sword Books Archaeology, Atlas, Aviation, Battleground, Discovery, Family History, History, Maritime, Military, Naval, Politics, Railways, Select, Transport, True Crime, Fiction, Frontline Books, Leo Cooper, Praetorian Press, Seaforth Publishing, Wharncliffe and White Owl.

For a complete list of Pen & Sword titles please contact

PEN & SWORD BOOKS LIMITED
47 Church Street, Barnsley, South Yorkshire, S70 2AS, England
E-mail: enquiries@pen-and-sword.co.uk
Website: www.pen-and-sword.co.uk

or

PEN AND SWORD BOOKS
1950 Lawrence Rd, Havertown, PA 19083, USA
E-mail: Uspen-and-sword@casematepublishers.com
Website: www.penandswordbooks.com

Introduction

This gallery of photographs aims to portray the atmosphere of Great Western Railway/British Railways (Western Region) branch lines from the early 1900s through to 1965. Not every line covered would necessarily be considered a branch line, but the trains depicted are generally branch line type services even when they are operating on more significant lines (e.g. the Chalford push and pull auto trains on the Gloucester-Swindon route).

The emphasis of this book is pictorial and captions have been kept to a minimum. Line history is barely covered because this information can usually be found on the Internet and in relevant books. Efforts have been made to find photographs which are not on the Internet and preferably featuring lesser-known stations and halts which generally have been rarely photographed. Where better known stations are depicted, more unusual views are shown wherever possible. Also, with only very few exceptions, the stations and halts feature trains but without these obscuring too much of the station infrastructure.

It would be impossible in a book such as this to portray every single GWR/BR(W) branch line and, in order to pursue the objective of using lesser-known/previously unseen/unusual pictures, some lines are favoured with several images while others have been omitted.

Most of the photographs have been provided by the Great Western Trust based at the Great Western Society's Didcot Railway Centre and by the Online Transport Archive, a charity which preserves transport prints, slides and film.

Monochrome images have been arranged geographically as far as possible, starting in the London area and proceeding westwards to Cornwall, then to the Dean Forest area, followed by the Midlands and ending up in Wales, proceeding westwards and then northwards. A separate colour section starts on page 101. The spelling of Welsh place names is generally that which was in use at the time when the photographs were taken.

Kevin R. McCormack
Ashtead, Surrey
April 2023

The Greenford branch, leaving the West of England main line at West Ealing, had three halts. This is South Greenford Halt with pannier tank No 8465 demonstrating the power of these post-war Hawksworth engines as it hauls a long goods train towards Greenford. For the period April 2019 to March 2020, South Greenford was London's least used railway station. See also page 101. (Bill Piggott)

The freight-only Brentford Dock branch from Southall (with the engine shed visible in the background of this view) lost its passenger services in 1942 and its only intermediate station, Trumpers Crossing Halte, closed in 1926. The line was singled in 1956 and the Dock closed in 1964, resulting in the branch being cut back to Brentford Town goods yard. Today, the line is still open and is famous for Windmill Bridge (nicknamed 'Three Bridges'), Brunel's last project completed two years before his death in 1859. (Author)

Large prairie tank No 6151 stands at Windsor & Eton Central station in 1959 with a through train to Paddington. This branch from Slough is still open today but the terminus, which originally had four platforms, now has just one short platform for 3-coach trains. The remainder of the station has been turned into a shopping mall. In this view a platform lighting replacement scheme is taking place. Windsor Castle is visible behind the left hand station canopy. (Marcus Eavis/ Online Transport Archive)

The last steam auto train to operate close to the London area was the **Marlow Donkey** *which worked from Maidenhead to Marlow via the Wycombe line to Bourne End, with some services to High Wycombe. The first station was Furze Platt Halt where the arrival of Collett 14xx 0-4-2 tank No 1448 is clearly welcomed in this late 1950s view. The halt was opened in 1937 to serve Maidenhead's increasing population, 83 years after the Wycombe line itself was built. (Great Western Trust)*

This is the original Italianate style Marlow station, with the water tower and engine shed visible on the left. On the right of the locomotive is the goods shed. In the latter days of steam operation, the auto train was normally propelled into the terminus which facilitated the collection of any freight vehicles, these being tagged on behind the auto trailer. In this view, the train hauled by No 1448 is facing in the opposite direction. See also page 101. (Great Western Trust)

Bourne End North signal box is showing evidence of past enlargement in this view of the level crossing in Station Road. The closure of the Wycombe line from Maidenhead beyond Bourne End on 4 May 1970, combined with the removal of the level crossing once the tracks no longer extended beyond the station platforms, rendered a large manned signal box superfluous. It was closed in August 1971 and demolished. See also page 102. (Great Western Trust)

The Wycombe Railway extended its line from Maidenhead and High Wycombe to Thame via Princes Risborough in 1862 and added the Thame-Kennington Junction (for Oxford) section two years later. Here is large prairie tank No 4148 entering Bledlow, the first station beyond Princes Risborough. The building (now extended) and platform are still extant in Sandpit Lane, next to the Phoenix Trail. (Great Western Trust)

This photograph was taken on 6 January 1963, the final day of passenger services on the Princes Risborough-Oxford branch. Having passed under Thame's distinctive train shed roof large prairie tank No 6111 takes water on its journey to Princes Risborough in extremely wintry conditions. (Author)

Large prairie tank No 6123 enters Tiddington station, located between Thame and Wheatley on the Princes Risborough-Oxford branch. This was one of three branches operating from Princes Risborough (see below and page 102). (Great Western Trust)

The Princes Risborough-Aylesbury branch is still open and on the last day of steam operation (Sunday 27 June 1962) the engine crew decorated their steed (0-4-2 tank No 1440). A school friend and I had travelled from Ealing to Princes Risborough and found ourselves stranded at Aylesbury after 1440 dropped off its auto trailer, Thrush, to return light engine. The kindly driver took pity on us and gave us a cab ride to Princes Risborough, with streamers and union flag still attached. (Author)

This was my first sighting (aged 14) of a 'sandwiched' locomotive as pannier tank No 5420 propels auto trailer W221 Wren (previously a regular combination on the Greenford branch) while pulling a former Southern Railway PC34 utility van. The train is leaving Princes Risborough for Aylesbury on 17 April 1961. Note the combination of upper and lower quadrant signals. (Author)

A useful north/south rail link, particularly for freight traffic from the Midlands to the English Channel, was the Didcot, Newbury and Southampton Railway (DN&S). The first station south of Didcot was Upton & Blewbury, seen here featuring 1897-built Duke of Cornwall 4-4-0 No 3281 Fowey (later becoming 3272 and 9072) but nameless since 1930. The station closed on 10 September 1962 when passenger services were withdrawn on the upper section of the line and is now a private residence (with matching extension) situated in Beeching Close, off Station Road. (Great Western Trust)

A railway journey from Didcot to Oxford takes travellers through Radley station which was the junction for the 1.75 mile Abingdon branch. In this c.1920s view, a 517 class 0-4-2 tank attached to a Churchward auto trailer has arrived from Radley. The similar looking 14XX 0-4-2 tanks represented an updated version of the 517s and started to replace their predecessors in the 1930s. Passenger services on the branch were withdrawn on 9 September 1963. See also page 103. (Great Western Trust)

The initial section of the Oxford-Fairford branch opened from Yarnton Junction to Witney in 1861 but Cassington Halt, the first station after Yarnton, was not built until 1936 and was later moved to the position seen here on the opposite side of the adjacent A40 overbridge. In this view, pannier tank No 9640 is speeding through with a freight. Notice the brick steps beside the lamp posts to enable the oil lamps on this unstaffed halt to be lit by the train guard. (Great Western Trust)

No 9640 has now arrived at Witney goods yard, the location of the original passenger station until the line was extended to Fairford and a new through station constructed (see page 103). Freight services to Witney continued until 2 November 1970, eight years after the Fairford section was closed. (Great Western Trust)

Fairford was built as a through station in anticipation of the line continuing to Cirencester and connecting with the Midland & South Western Junction Railway (MSWJR). However, this plan never materialised and Fairford became a remotely situated terminus. In this scene, 2251 class 0-6-0 No 2252 stands alongside the engine shed while pannier tank No 9652 takes on water after being turned. Passenger services on the branch were withdrawn on 18 June 1962. (Great Western Trust)

Marlborough once had two passenger stations serving the town. These belonged to the GWR and the MSWJR, the latter being merged with the GWR at the Grouping. The GWR station was closed to passengers in 1933 and its Savernake to Marlborough branch trains rerouted into the former MSWJR station. Closure to passengers occurred in 1961 and to freight in 1964. Here, pannier tank No 9721 has arrived from Savernake, located on the main line between Newbury and Westbury. (Great Western Trust)

Newbury, on the West of England main line from Reading, was a junction not only for the line from Didcot to Southampton but also for the Lambourn branch. One of the intermediate stations at the Lambourn end was East Garston, seen here being visited by pannier tank No 4606. The Lambourn Valley Railway opened in 1898 and subsequently bought three locomotives. However, mounting debts forced the Company to sell its engines in 1904 in favour of using hired steam railmotors from the GWR which went on to acquire the line in the following year. See also page 104. (Great Western Trust)

New Passage, opened in 1928 and named after the ferry which used to cross the Severn Estuary from South Gloucestershire to South Wales, was on a line from Bristol Temple Meads through Avonmouth to Pilning. The local line now terminates at Severn Beach and the section which included New Passage closed to passengers on 23 November 1964. Here we see a Bristol-bound train hauled by small prairie tank No 5509. (Great Western Trust)

Sandford and Banwell was a station on the Cheddar Valley line which opened in 1869 and closed to passengers on 9 September 1963. The station has been preserved and looks much as it does in this photograph of small prairie tank No 5553 (also preserved). A section of track has been laid at the platform on which a carriage and two trucks have been positioned. (Great Western Trust)

After Sandford and Banwell on the Cheddar Valley railway (the so-called Strawberry Line) came Winscombe but fortune has not favoured the station which has been demolished nor the locomotive (No 5559) which was not blessed with a return ticket to Woodhams scrapyard at Barry but was sent elsewhere for scrapping. However, the platform at Winscombe has been reinstated with railings and GWR benches installed. **(Great Western Trust)**

Travelling some distance south we reach Wells, where GWR diesel railcar W28 is standing. This station started and ended life with the name of Wells but from 1920 to 1951 it carried the appendage of Tucker Street to distinguish it from the former Somerset & Dorset Railway station at Priory Road. A section of the Cheddar Valley line around Cranmore (between Shepton Mallet and Witham) has become the East Somerset heritage railway. **(R.W. Jones/Online Transport Archive)**

Four branch lines originated at Taunton in Somerset and none forms part of today's national rail network, although one has become a heritage railway. This picture is a view of Lyng Halt situated at the Taunton end of the line to Yeovil between Durston (on the Bristol-Exeter mainline) and Athelney. It opened in 1928 and closed on 15 June 1964 along with the remainder of the branch to Yeovil. (Great Western Trust)

The longest of Taunton's defunct branch lines was the one to Barnstaple, a cross-country route some 43 miles in length. Consequently, in steam days, trains were normally hauled by tender engines, latterly GWR mogul 2-6-0s of the 4300 class. The second intermediate station from Taunton was Wiveliscombe where No 6375 was photographed. The last BR(W) passenger train ran on 1 October 1966. See also page 106. (Great Western Trust)

Dulverton, located two miles from the town at Brushford, was the largest intermediate station on the Taunton-Barnstable line because it was also the terminus of the Exe Valley branch from Exeter via Tiverton. In this early scene, a Barnstaple-bound train prepares to leave, probably headed by a class 455 Metro 2-4-0 tank. The station building and goods shed survive today, visible from the B 3222 at Brushford. (Great Western Trust)

Another former branch line emanating from Taunton was the Chard branch (see also pages 107-8). This photograph was taken to depict the GWR enamel notice and pannier tank No 3787 taking water at Chard Central rather than the local children (one with a bow and arrow) playing on the railway and reluctant to move out of the way! **(Author)**

No 3787 leaves the dereliction of Chard Central for Chard Junction, with bow and arrow boy trying to outrun the train, provoking memories of carefree childhood days of yore, reminiscent of the book and film **The Railway Children.** **(Author)**

The fourth Taunton branch line was the one to Minehead which was closed on 4 January 1971 and reopened by the heritage West Somerset Railway on 28 March 1976. In this view, pannier tank No 9764 stands at Watchet station bound for Taunton. When BR closed the line it was kept intact, resulting in the infrastructure seen here remaining in place including the 1862 goods shed (behind the train) which is now the Watchet Boat Museum. (Great Western Trust)

A goods train headed by a Dean Goods 0-6-0 trundles through Blue Anchor, the second intermediate station east of Minehead, consisting of wagons and vans belonging to various railway companies and a private owner. Blue Anchor station, located alongside the beach, opened in 1874 when the line was extended beyond the original terminus at Watchet. (Great Western Trust)

Bishops Lydeard is the normal eastern terminus of the heritage West Somerset Railway (WSR) about twenty miles from Minehead, although some special services continue to the WSR's own station at Norton Fitzwarren. This picture depicts a small prairie tank on a Taunton-bound train. (Great Western Trust)

On the Exe Valley line, there was a slaughter house adjacent to Tiverton station and this photograph taken from the signal box around 1935 depicts the 'Meat Train' about to take the branch to Tiverton Junction pulled by a Hall class locomotive. On weekdays, the meat vans were added to the normal evening goods train but on Sundays it was a special working, as seen here. (Porter Swatridge)

How not to fill up a locomotive's tank: turn on the water and abandon the engine! 0-4-2 tank No 1450 (since preserved) has temporarily uncoupled from its auto trailers at Dulverton and has a drink before propelling an Exe Valley train back to Tiverton and Exeter. (Author)

This is an example of the correct way to take on water, as demonstrated by the fireman of remarkably clean pannier tank No 3659 at Tiverton on an Exeter to Dulverton non-auto-train in August 1962, a journey of almost 25 miles. See also page 108. (Author)

This Tiverton picture depicts the 'Tivvy Bumper' waiting to depart for Tiverton Junction hauled by 0-4-2 tank No 1469. Note that the glazed platform canopies seen on page 21 have been replaced by much plainer ones. The station was built as a terminus for the Tiverton Junction branch in 1848 and was reconstructed as a through station when the Exe Valley line arrived in 1884/5. (Great Western Trust)

How to fill one's billycan with boiling water to make tea! No 1450, standing in one of the 'Tivvy Bumper' bay platforms at Tiverton went on to haul the last passenger train on the Tiverton-Tiverton Junction branch on 3 October 1964. (Author)

This is Halberton Halt, the only intermediate station between Tiverton and Tiverton Junction, which opened in 1927. In August 1962, I obtained a ride from Tiverton Junction to Tiverton in the driver's compartment of the auto trailer which was being propelled by No 1466. The driver spent the journey chatting to me rather than operating the regulator and told me that the fireman (on the footplate) was driving. So, no actual auto working was taking place! (Author)

Tiverton Junction was also the mainline terminus of the Hemyock branch, originally known as the Culm Valley Light Railway. Seemingly visiting a farmyard, 0-4-2 tank No 1451 is actually standing at Whitehall Halt. This was the first stop on the branch and the last to be built in 1933, the line having opened in 1876. Passenger services were withdrawn on 9 September 1963 but milk traffic for the dairy at Hemyock continued until 31 October 1975. (Author)

Exeter was a junction for two GWR branches: the Exe Valley line to Dulverton (see pages 22 & 108) and the Teign Valley line which joined the Newton Abbot-Moretonhampstead branch at Heathfield. As with the Exe Valley, the Teign Valley line was built in two halves initially by separate companies and Christow, seen here with Churchward auto trailers in the platforms, was the original terminus of the line from Heathfield. (Great Western Trust)

Whereas passenger services on the Exeter-Christow part of the Teign Valley line were withdrawn on 9 June 1958, passenger services on the remaining section continued until 1 May 1961. Today there is an embryonic Exeter & Teign Valley Railway based in the former goods yard at Christow which hopes to reopen the line. This picture depicts small prairie tank No 5530 at another of the intermediate stations, Trusham. (Great Western Trust)

This is Bovey station, the first one north of Heathfield, on the Moretonhampstead branch which closed to passengers on 2 March 1959 (see also page 109). A new alignment of the A382 road now occupies the trackbed here but the station building and goods shed survive (the former is the Bovey Tracey Heritage Centre) standing at the side of the road following the removal of the platform. (Great Western Trust)

Six-wheeler No 9987 stands at Lustleigh, between Bovey and Moretonhampstead, in 1935. This carriage was originally No 791, built in 1884 as a 5-compartment composite (i.e. providing mixed classes) under Diagram U19. It later became No 6791 and was converted into a camping coach in 1934, the first year that the GWR introduced these popular holiday facilities. (Great Western Trust)

Just south of Newton Abbot the main line split to create a branch line to Torquay, Paignton and Kingswear. From a National Rail perspective, the branch (part of today's Riviera Line) now terminates at Paignton and the Dartmouth Steam Railway operates the remaining section to Kingswear. This picture was taken in 1932 at Torquay and shows No 5571 heading a down train to Kingswear. The station as seen here was completed in 1878 and is Grade II Listed. (Author's collection)

In the inter-war years, the public relied heavily on trains to take them to their holiday destinations, as evidenced by the huge amount of luggage piled up on the platform at Paignton. The station is largely unchanged today (apart from the absence of luggage and the small prairie tank engines) but the goods yard on the left is now occupied by the Dartmouth Steam Railway for its services to Kingswear and ferry to Dartmouth. BR sold the Kingswear section to the Dart Valley Light Railway at the end of 1972. (Great Western Trust)

Roughly midway between Paignton and Kingwear is Churston which was the junction for the 2-mile branch to Brixham. 0-4-2 tank No 1466 is featured here at Churston on the last day of passenger services, 11 May 1963. The Dartmouth Steam Railway's carriage workshop now stands on the site of this branch bay platform. (Great Western Trust)

Two Collett main line coaches stand at the end of the platform at Kingswear in this late 1930s photograph. They are probably waiting to be hauled to Paddington by King class locomotive No 6003 **King George IV** which is occupying the turntable road, having been turned. In the distance a local train is approaching hauled by a small prairie tank. (Great Western Trust)

0-4-2 tank No 1466 was based in the West Country for its entire service career from 1936 to 1963 and at the start of its preserved life. On 2 December 1967 it steamed to Didcot with No 6998 Burton Agnes Hall and miscellaneous rolling stock, creating an extraordinary train on which I travelled. Here is No 1466 at Ashburton, terminus of the 9-mile branch from Totnes which closed to passengers on 3 November 1958 and to goods in September 1962. The Dart Valley Light Railway (since succeeded by the South Devon Railway) subsequently acquired the line. (Great Western Trust)

This is Buckfastleigh, the current terminus of the South Devon Railway's heritage line from Totnes. Trains cannot run further because the trackbed from Buckfastleigh to Ashburton has been used for road improvement (A38) and the future of Ashburton station, with its train shed roof, has become uncertain over recent years. It is currently used as a car repair establishment (Station Garage) in Chuley Road. (Great Western Trust)

This delightful Edwardian picture was taken at Yelverton on the Plymouth to Launceston branch. The main station building was angled because it also served the Princetown branch which started at Yelverton in front of the trees on the right and had an intermediate station at Dousland (mentioned on the station sign on the far left). The GW wagon striking an unusual pose on the extreme right is standing at the end of the turntable road for the Princetown branch. This line closed on 5 March 1956 and the Launceston branch closed on 31 December 1962. In this photograph, the train engine is 3521 class 4-4-0 No 3551 which was built as a Broad Gauge 'convertible' 0-4-2 saddle tank in 1888, altered to 0-4-4 wheel arrangement in 1890 to improve stability (but still prone to derailment), converted to standard gauge in 1892 and later rebuilt as a 4-4-0 tender engine. (Great Western Trust)

This is Plym Bridge Platform in its original form with small prairie tank No 5519 approaching with a train to Launceston. When opened in 1906 the station was called Plym Bridge Halt but was soon redesignated Plym Bridge Platform. It was reopened by the heritage Plym Valley Railway on 30 December 2012, exactly fifty years to the day after the last BR(W) train departed. See also pages 110-111. (Great Western Trust)

Marytavy and Blackdown station on the Launceston branch looks somewhat neglected when visited here by small prairie tank No 5519. Originally there were two platforms serving both GWR and LSWR trains, but the latter company ceased using the branch in 1890 when it opened its own line between Tavistock and Lydford. The signal box looks in reasonable condition considering it closed in August 1894! (Great Western Trust)

No 5551 brings a short freight from Moorswater yard towards Coombe Junction after passing under the Moorswater viaduct carrying the Plymouth-Penzance mainline. This viaduct was completed in 1881, replacing Brunel's 1859 timber version, the masonry piers of which are visible here and which are Grade II* Listed along with the present structure. (Great Western Trust)

4500 class small prairie No 4565 has arrived at the Looe branch station at Liskeard. The engine will now run round its train for the return journey, a manoeuvre which it will have to repeat when it descends the loop to reach Coombe Junction Halt. The branch is still open, as is the station shown here. (Great Western Trust)

A 4575 class small prairie tank pulls in to St Keyne (for St Keyne Well) on the Looe branch. This station opened in 1902 soon after the opening of the Liskeard loop. St Keyne has now been rebranded St Keyne Wishing Well Halt, currently one of only two stations on National Rail to be suffixed 'Halt' (the second being Coombe Junction), others having lost this appellation by 1974. The corrugated iron shelter has since been replaced by an appropriate old-style structure. (Great Western Trust)

Looe was an unusual terminus in not having a turning loop in the station. This was situated beyond, in the goods yard to which the train has been signalled to advance, having deposited its passengers. The hut on the right was the signal box. Looe Police Station has now been built on the site of the former station building. As a result, the terminus has been pushed back a short distance and a smaller station building constructed. (Great Western Trust)

Westwards from Liskeard is Bodmin Road (now Parkway) which was the junction for the branch to Bodmin General, seen here festooned with advertisements in this inter-war picture. The station was also the terminus of the line from Padstow via Boscarne Junction, both routes closing on 30 January 1967. The Great Western Society (GWS) then created a depot there in May 1969, following the transfer of saddletank No 1363 from the GWS site at Totnes. This engine moved to Didcot in 1977 and the site was vacated, only to be occupied later by the Bodmin & Wenford heritage railway. (Great Western Trust)

Beyond Bodmin Road is Lostwithiel, which was the junction for the Fowey branch and was latterly a regular haunt for 0-4-2 tank No 1419, seen here at Fowey. This station was also reached by a branch from St Blazey via Par which closed in 1968 and has been converted into a private Haul Road. Regular passenger services on the latter line ceased much earlier, in 1928. See also page 111. (Great Western Trust)

A mineral branch accessed from the Par-Newquay line ran from St Dennis Junction to Burngullow on the Cornish mainline. It never carried passengers and the St Dennis- Parkandillack section closed in 1960. The branch remains open from Parkandillock/Drinnick Mill southwards for china clay trains to Par and Fowey docks. This picture depicts pannier tank No 7715 leaving the branch with a freight largely composed of filled china clay wagons. Some remains of Burngullow station, which closed in 1931, are visible on the left. See also page 112. (Great Western Trust)

A branch which remains open is the one from Truro to Falmouth Docks. One intermediate station is Penmere Platform which is beautifully maintained by the Friends of Penmere Station. The platform buildings in this picture were removed in the 1960s but there is now a shelter of traditional appearance in their place. There are GWR seats on the platform and the Penmere Platform running-in board on the extreme right is still fixed to the supports made out of old rails. No 5562 would not feel out of place there today. (Great Western Trust)

A small prairie tank leaves Falmouth station (out of view beyond the signal box along with the docks branch) on its way to Truro during the inter-war period. This section of line was closed to local passenger trains from 1970 to 1975 when a more centrally located halt was opened which was initially named Falmouth before becoming The Dell and later Falmouth Town. The previous Falmouth station was then reopened and called Falmouth Docks. (Author's collection)

Newquay was also reached by a branch from Chacewater which closed completely on 4 February 1963. One of the intermediate stations was St Agnes, seen here with a steam railmotor. These were introduced in 1905 outside the busy holiday season and new halts created. In 1937, St Agnes station was remodelled with an island platform and a passing loop. The station building became detached and the doorways on the platform side sealed. The canopy was removed and fitted to the opposite side of the building where it remains to this day. Passengers reached the platform from the station building by footbridge and later by crossing the track. (Great Western Trust)

Mithian Halt was one of the halts created for the steam railmotor services, opening on 14 August 1905. Following closure, the halt has since vanished. The locomotive featured in the photograph is small prairie tank No 5539 which was withdrawn in April 1962 and was lucky to be despatched to Woodham's scrapyard at Barry. It is currently under restoration, having been one of the 'Barry Ten' locomotives unsold when the scrapyard closed in 1990. (Great Western Trust)

Perranporth Beach Halt was the last station to be built on the line, Perranporth station itself being some distance from the beach which was popular with visitors. The halt opened in July 1931 and after the branch closed most of the concrete sections supporting the platform were reused for The Dell station (now Falmouth Town) on the Truro-Falmouth branch. (Great Western Trust)

The principal intermediate station on the Truro/Chacewater-Newquay branch was Perranporth. Access for passengers from the road to the island platform was by subway. Small Prairie No 5546 has arrived with three BR carriages. The locomotive was allocated to Truro depot (83F) but for only twelve months (July 1959–July 1960) and was withdrawn soon after (September 1960). (Great Western Trust)

No 5559 arrives at Shepherds with a short freight from the Newquay direction, probably waiting to pass another service as the driver is seated on the platform. When the train proceeds beyond the end of the platform it will pass the trackbed of the Treamble mineral line, last used in 1949, built to serve the iron ore mines at Gravel Hill and later the military Penhale training camp. No 5559 was based at Truro shed from October 1958 until withdrawal in January 1960. (Great Western Trust)

A train for Helston stands at Gwinear Road, one of seventeen stations subsequently closed on the Plymouth to Penzance mainline. It became a junction in 1887 when the Helston branch opened. This 8.5 mile branch closed to passengers on 3 September 1962 and to freight on 5 October 1964. The Helston Railway Preservation Society has reopened a 1.5 mile section and hopes to extend to a total of 3 miles. (Great Western Trust)

Helston, seen here in 1959, was designed as a through station in preparation for an extension to The Lizard but the GWR, which had bought the line in 1898, decided to avoid the capital costs of railway construction by introducing a motor bus service instead, the first such operation. Since the branch closed the station has been replaced by housing but the Goods Shed is still standing as part of a Community Centre in Station Road. (Great Western Trust)

The most westerly branch in Cornwall is the St Erth-St Ives line which is 4.25 miles long and remains open today. One of the intermediate stations, now a request stop, is Lelant which is on the edge of the Hayle Estuary. The station building has been converted into a private house with a sympathetic extension. In steam days, 44XX small prairie tanks were used from 1904 but the heavier 4500 class were subsequently given a dispensation to operate. Normally the 4575 class was banned, although exceptions did occur providing the locomotive water tanks were not completely filled. (Great Western Trust)

In my early train-spotting days I would often ask the engine crew if they would let me onto the footplate. When I visited the branch aged 14 on 25 July 1961, the kind driver offered me a ride from St Ives station to the small engine shed on No 4563 and I took this picture as a reminder. The shed closed just a few weeks later in September 1961 when DMUs took over. It has since been demolished, as has the original station. A replacement station was opened in May 1971 on the site of the goods shed, resulting in a slight shortening of the branch similar to the situation at Looe (see page 33). (Author)

Leaving the furthest reaches of Cornwall we head to the Forest of Dean. The Wye Valley Railway ran from Chepstow to Monmouth, two Welsh towns, but the line straddled the England/Wales border. The first station beyond Chepstow heading north was Tidenham in West Gloucestershire where auto pannier tank No 6412 has just arrived (the engine was later purchased for preservation direct from BR). Passenger services were withdrawn on 5 January 1959, but the goods siding was closed in February 1955. (Great Western Trust)

This panoramic view of Coleford shows its two railway stations (since demolished) and probably dates from summer 1950 when two railtours were run. This would account for the streamlined diesel railcar, believed to be W7, standing at the former Severn & Wye Railway station on the right. This station, terminus of a branch from Parkend (now on the heritage Dean Forest Railway), closed to passengers in 1924. On the far left is the GWR station, terminus of passenger services from Monmouth which ceased in 1917. In the centre is the Goods Shed which survives as the Coleford Great Western Museum. (R.W. Jones/Online Transport Archive)

The rail network in the Forest of Dean area was complex as a result of companies vying with each other to reach the rich mineral deposits. Ruspidge Halt was located on the Bullo Pill branch to Bilson and Cinderford which closed on 3 November 1958 and this view depicts light pannier tank No 1639 entering the platform. Part of this is still extant with an identical replica running-in board, along with a signal and a tank wagon. The public can sit on GWR replica seats and use their imagination, but the station building has not survived. (Great Western Trust)

The former Ross and Monmouth Railway linking Ross-on-Wye in Herefordshire and Monmouth in Wales passed through Symonds Yat in the Wye Valley where this picture of an auto train hauled by 0-4-2 tank No 1455 was taken. The line closed on 5 January 1959 and no trace remains of the station which is now the site of an hotel car park. (R.W. Jones/Online Transport Archive)

Another intermediate station on the Ross-on-Wye–Monmouth line was Kerne Bridge. It may look busy in this picture but the carriage on the left is a Camping Coach standing in a siding which was once a passing loop. Now a private house, the station building is sandwiched between two large extensions. (Great Western Trust)

Monmouth Troy was the junction for lines to Ross-on-Wye, Coleford, Chepstow and Pontypool Road in South Wales (the latter accessed via the tunnel in the background). Consequently, it could become a busy station with branch line services often consisting of steam-hauled auto trains. GWR diesel railcars could also be seen, as pictured here on a particularly wet day. (R.W. Jones/Online Transport Archive)

We return to Gloucestershire for the next series of pictures, starting with two branch lines which left the Swindon to Gloucester line at Kemble. This is the Tetbury terminus on a wet day, located 7.5 miles from Kemble, with pannier tank No 7794 at the head of a mixed train. The branch closed on 6 April 1964 and the station building was demolished. However, the large Goods Shed behind the freight wagons remains, having been converted into an arts centre. (R.W. Jones/Online Transport Archive)

In an unsuccessful attempt to revitalise the Tetbury branch, diesel railbuses were introduced from 2 February 1959 and two new halts created, one of which was outside the Trouble House hostelry seen in the background. The halt was built specifically to serve the inn which is located in a remote area on the A433 road. The inn opened in 1754 and acquired its current name in the late 1800s, reputedly following a series of misfortunes associated with it. (Great Western Trust)

The 5-mile branch to Cirencester was the second one originating from Kemble and closed for passengers on the same day as the Tetbury branch but goods traffic was not withdrawn until 4 October 1965. There are currently proposals to rebuild the line as a Community Railway using very light railcars. This picture of pannier tank No 7418 from Swindon shed (82C) pre-dates the introduction of the diesel railbuses in February 1959. See also page 113. (Great Western Trust)

There used to be a through line from Banbury to Cheltenham. The eastern section from Chipping Norton to Kings Sutton (for Banbury) closed to passengers in 1951 and to freight in 1958 while the middle section, from Kingham to Chipping Norton lasted until 3 December 1962. This part of the line had only one intermediate station, Sarsden Halt, as seen here with small prairie tank No 4573, a locomotive allocated to Gloucester (Horton Road) from 1956 to 1960. The signal box dates from 1893. See also page 113. (Great Western Trust)

Rushwick station was on the Worcester-Hereford line, situated between Worcester (Foregate Street) and Leominster Junction. This route to Hereford via Great Malvern and Ledbury remains open but many of the intermediate stations have been closed including Rushwick which succumbed on 5 April 1965. Here is a local southbound train headed by pannier tank No 4664. See also page 115. (Great Western Trust)

This is one of the GWR's streamlined diesel railcars which were numbered 1-18. The vehicle is operating on the Worcester-Bromyard branch which closed to passengers on 7 September 1964. The line originally extended to Leominster but that section from Bromyard closed to passengers on 15 September 1952. Knightwick station was located on the Worcester-Bromyard section and has since been converted into a private residence. (Great Western Trust)

Another station house which has become a private residence is the one whose chimney stack appears to be protruding from the roof of GWR diesel railcar No W20W. Withdrawn in 1962, this vehicle has been preserved by the Kent & East Sussex Railway and hauled their first revenue-earning train in February 1974. Newnham Bridge station was on the former Tenbury and Bewdley Railway and closed on 1 August 1962. (Great Western Trust)

Burlish Halt, seen here being visited by a GWR diesel railcar with 'speed whiskers', was situated on the Bewdley to Hartlebury 'triangle'. The halt opened in 1930 primarily to serve a local porcelain factory and closed on 6 January 1970. Prior to closure, the pagoda hut was replaced by a bus shelter and a modern running-in board installed. **(Great Western Trust)**

This GWR diesel railcar is running along track which now forms part of the heritage Severn Valley Railway (the Bewdley-Kidderminster section which reopened in 1984 and was previously known as the Bewdley Loop Line). Foley Park Halt had been moved from the opposite side of the line to its position seen here to allow space for sidings serving the British Sugar Factory. The halt closed on 6 January 1970 when passenger services were withdrawn on the Loop Line and has not been reopened. **(Great Western Trust)**

Radiating from Bewdley were lines to Bridgnorth/Buildwas, Hartlebury/Droitwich, Kidderminster/ Stourbridge Junction and Tenbury Wells/Woofferton. The first two sections mentioned above originally provided a through service from Shrewsbury to Worcester. In this view at Bewdley, large prairie tank No 6118 is working a train towards Kidderminster. This class was normally associated with the London division but No 6118 was based at Tyseley (Birmingham) from 1953 to 1958 and then moved to Wales. See also page 115. (Great Western Trust)

Rear views of steam locomotives are not the prettiest of sights, least of all when the subject is a Standard class 3 2-6-2 tank. This one is coming to a stop at Northwood Halt, just north of Bewdley, which closed on 9 September 1963. It is now an unstaffed request stop on the heritage Severn Valley Railway, making it the only surviving original halt on the line. The wooden platform shelter in this picture has been replaced by a GWR pagoda hut. (Great Western Trust)

Standard class 3 2-6-2 tank No 82004 pulls in to Highley station on what is now the heritage Severn Valley Railway. The mineral truck serves as a reminder that there were several collieries in the area, the last of which, Alveley, closed in 1969, bringing an end to freight traffic at Highley. The station only had one platform and the additional two tracks were used for freight traffic. The lattice girder bridge in the background has since been replaced by one of similar design. **(Great Western Trust)**

Continuing our journey northwards on the Severn Valley Railway from Highley we come to another restored and reopened station, Hampton Loade. Here it is in the pre-preservation era with Standard tank No 82032 arriving from Bridgnorth, probably with a Shrewsbury-Worcester train. The locomotive was in service for only ten years (1955-65) and was allocated to Shrewsbury shed from 1961-64. **(Great Western Trust)**

There is a mountain of freight being loaded into, or unloaded from, this GWR diesel railcar at Bridgnorth which is signalled to head northwards towards Buildwas. Also, the goods yard looks to be particularly busy. Bridgnorth is now the northern terminus of the heritage Severn Valley Railway and the main engine shed and works occupy the goods yard site. (Great Western Trust)

Beyond Bridgnorth, on the now abandoned northern part of the former Severn Valley line, is Coalport station, which closed on 9 September 1963. A train from Shrewsbury is entering the station hauled by small prairie tank No 5518 which spent from 1951-4 and 1956-60 allocated to Kidderminster shed (85D). All the buildings seen here as well as the platforms are still extant and two BR Mk I coaches stand on a short piece of track which are available for holiday rental. (Great Western Trust)

Between Coalport and Ironbridge stood Jackfield Halt. The original halt was opened in 1934 but in 1954 the platform and track slid towards the River Severn due to land subsidence. The halt was therefore resited but the ground at the new location also proved unstable. It was not until 2016 that the problem was rectified but no trace now remains of the halt. This view depicts an approaching train hauled by a Standard class 3 tank. (Great Western Trust)

Standard class 3 tank No 82000 based at Shrewsbury from December 1955 to January 1959 enters Iron-Bridge and Broseley. The station site is now a car park but there are currently ambitious proposals to reinstate ten miles of the northern section of the Severn Valley line from Buildwas to Bridgnorth which would vastly improve transport links to the Ironbridge World Heritage Site. (Great Western Trust)

Buildwas connected the former Severn Valley Railway to the Craven Arms to Wellington line. One of the stations on the latter line was Much Wenlock and passenger services from there to Wellington (Shropshire) were withdrawn on 23 July 1962 and the station closed. The section from Much Wenlock to Craven Arms had closed to passengers as early as 1951. Pannier tank No 3760 was allocated to Wellington (84H) from September 1950 to November 1958. The station building survives as a private dwelling. (Great Western Trust)

The first station on the section from Buildwas to Wellington was Coalbrookdale, where pannier tank No 9639 is seen in this view. The Italianate station building on the left survives and the tracks are still in situ because freight services continued here until 2015 when Ironbridge B power station at Buildwas closed. The Telford Steam Railway based at Horsehay & Dawley has ambitions to extend its line through Coalbrookdale to Ironbridge and across to Madeley Junction, thereby connecting with the Shrewsbury-Wolverhampton main line. (Great Western Trust)

Lightmoor was on the Craven Arms-Wellington line, a short section of which is operated by the heritage Telford Steam Railway, and also on the Ironbridge branch from Buildwas to Madeley Junction which is currently mothballed by Network Rail. Prospective passengers stand ready to board this train headed by a large prairie tank. It is possible that passenger trains will once more return to Lightmoor. *(Great Western Trust)*

We leave the Craven Arms-Wellington line near its upper end with this view of Ketley Town Halt which opened in 1936. Pulling in to the halt is large prairie tank No 4110 which was shedded at Wellington from December 1956 to September 1959. On withdrawal in June 1965, the engine was fortuitously sent to Woodhams scrapyard at Barry. Now owned by the Dartmouth Steam Railway it is currently being restored to service by the East Somerset Railway, having been non-operational since 1965. *(Great Western Trust)*

Old Hill station, although much altered, is still open for services to Birmingham, but the branch to Halesowen mentioned on the running-in board closed to passengers as far back as 1927 except for workmen's trains which lasted until 1958. The branch from Old Hill to Dudley (the 'Bumble Hole' branch, a name applied to an area around the Dudley Canal at Windmill End, one of the intermediate stations) did not close to passengers until 15 June 1964 (and to freight in January 1968). A 'Bumble Hole' auto train from Dudley is pictured here hauled by pannier tank No 6418. (Great Western Trust)

A diesel 'bubble car' crosses Station Road at Old Hill on the 'Bumble Hole' branch. This scene is almost unrecognisable today following the demolition of the bridge and realignment of the road. The houses through the bridge in Station Road are still standing (the remainder of Station Road is in the left foreground). Also, some of the small posts along the pavement and the brick pillar adjoining the gate post have survived. The car is emerging from Beauty Bank and the road heading to the right is Waterfall Lane. The Crown pub sign has been renewed. (Martin Jenkins/Online Transport Archive)

The section of the former Oxford, Worcester and Wolverhampton Railway between Dudley and Wolverhampton which closed to passengers on 30 July 1962 remained open for freight until 22 September 1968 but now no longer exists. Daisy Bank & Bradley, one of the intermediate stations, has also vanished without trace. In this view, a large prairie tank heads a southbound passenger train towards Dudley. (Great Western Trust)

Proceeding in a north westerly direction we head again to the England/Wales border area and visit the Llanfyllin branch. This ran from Llanymynech on the Whitchurch-Oswestry-Welshpool line which closed to passengers on 18 January 1965 along with the branch. Looking rather like Arnold Ridley's Ghost Train, Ivatt 2-6-0 No 46516 from Shrewsbury shed is entering Llanfechain station possibly on the last day of services, 16 January 1965. The station building is now a private residence. (E.C. Bennett & Martin Jenkins/Online Transport Archive)

This auto train is standing in Ellesmere station, Shropshire, which was located on the Whitchurch-Oswestry line and also served as a junction for the branch to Wrexham which is the destination of the service seen here. This was withdrawn on 10 September 1962, but the station remained open until passenger services on the Whitchurch-Oswestry line were withdrawn on 18 January 1965. The Grade II Listed station building has been converted into apartments and is located in Brownlow Road, adjacent to Brownlow Crescent. (Martin Jenkins/Online Transport Archive)

Another branch line in the upper border area was the one in Shropshire from Oswestry to Gobowen. This closed to passengers on 7 November 1966 and to freight in 1971. Cambrian Heritage Railways is based at the now closed station at Oswestry and the preservation society hopes eventually to reopen the line to Gobowen. This latter station is still open and is located on the Shrewsbury-Chester mainline. However, the bay platform occupied here by 0-4-2 tank No 1458 is disused and the footbridge has been removed. (E.C. Bennett & Martin Jenkins/Online Transport Archive)

Moving down to South Wales, we start with the line from Monmouth (Troy) to Pontypool Road. This line was originally built by the Coleford, Monmouth, Usk and Pontypool Railway for the transportation of iron ore from the Forest of Dean to the blast furnaces at Nantyglo, near Ebbw Vale. Passenger services were officially withdrawn on 13 June 1955, but the last day was 28 May 1955, due to a national railway strike. In the sylvan setting of Usk station, Pontypool Road-based 0-6-2 tank No 6693, probably heading a railtour, stands at the platform having emerged from Usk tunnel. The station buildings have since been demolished and the site has largely been reclaimed by undergrowth, but the tunnel has been converted into a footpath. (R.W. Jones/Online Transport Archive)

Usk possessed a large signal box which is seen here being visited by a Western Region 3-car suburban DMU set. The train carries the legend SPECIAL and it is believed that the picture was taken on 12 October 1957. This was the date of the Usk-Monmouth Centenary Railtour hauled by pannier tank No 4668 which was the last time a passenger train visited Usk. (R.W. Jones/ Online Transport Archive)

Cefntilla Halt, situated between Llandenny and Usk on the Pontypool-Monmouth line, had an operational life of little over a year. In the early 1950s, when passenger services were under threat, this halt was built in a vain attempt to increase passenger numbers. It opened on 27 March 1954 and closed when the last passenger train ran on 28 May 1955. (Great Western Trust)

Travelling to the Cardiff area we visit Grangetown, located about one mile south west of Cardiff Central. The island platform configuration dates from 1904 but the extensive canopy has now been replaced by a bus shelter. This photograph depicts pannier tank No 6438 working a Cardiff (Clarence Road)-Pontypridd service, colloquially known as the St Fagan's Pullman or the Pontypridd Flyer. The target code JB indicates that the locomotive hails from Abercynon and is working an auto train service. (Great Western Trust)

Small prairie tank No 5527 propels an auto train out of Wenvoe station, located between Creigau and Cadoxton, in summer 1958. The target code BG refers to a Barry shed auto train duty. Passenger services were withdrawn on 10 September 1962 and the main station building (on the far right) is now a private residence. No 5527 was one of fifteen 4575 class locos fitted for auto working in 1953 to operate in the Cardiff area. They were displaced in 1958 when DMUs took over many of the local services in the valleys. (R.W. Jones/Online Transport Archive)

Moving westwards along the South Wales coast brings us to the Porthcawl branch from Pyle. There was just one intermediate stop, Nottage Halt, which served the local village as well as Royal Porthcawl Golf Club. Built in the 1900s as an unadvertised halt for golfers it was named Nottage Halt in 1924 and became a public station. The branch was well patronised during the summer months as Porthcawl was a popular seaside resort so its closure to passengers on 9 September 1963 was particularly controversial. Collett 0-6-2 tank No 5631 was withdrawn in September 1962 and scrapped. (Great Western Trust)

The labyrinth of railway lines in South Wales makes a sequential geographical journey difficult. Heading eastwards inland brings us to the lower end of the former Brecon and Merthyr Railway. This is Bassaleg station on the western outskirts of Newport, not to be confused with nearby Bassaleg Junction. Both stations were closed to passengers on 31 December 1962 but a new one opened in 2014 near the Junction. In this view, pannier tank No 3638 is working a Newport-Brecon service. (Great Western Trust)

Welcome to Waterloo station! This one, situated on the Brecon & Merthyr Railway's Machen Loop to Caerphilly (see also page 117). contrasts significantly with its namesake in London. There is no raised platform or shelter and passengers had to wait in the fenced enclosure until the guard on an arriving train unlocked the entry gate. As explained in the next caption, trains ran in one direction only (to Caerphilly) and the Halt (although not named as such) closed on 17 September 1956 when Machen-Pontypridd passenger services were withdrawn. (R.W. Jones/Online Transport Archive)

On the opposite side of the Rhymney River stood Fountain Bridge Halt serving Up trains only. The reason for this alternative route (built by the Pontypridd Caerphilly and Newport Railway) was due to the very steep gradient out of Caerphilly which restricted the length of mineral trains. The new eastward line was built with a much easier gradient. Like Waterloo, Fountain Bridge Halt had no raised platform so the use of auto trailers with retractable steps operated by the guard were essential for passengers. Here is one such coach, hauled by No 6438. (R.W. Jones/Online Transport Archive)

West of Machen on the former Brecon & Merthyr Railway leading to Rhymney and Brecon was Bedwas station, after which the line turned northwards. This view looking westwards depicts a train hauled by pannier tank No 9616. This engine had a short service life of just under twenty years, spending almost all of that time allocated to Ebbw Junction shed at Newport (86A). At the end of the main platform, a somersault signal can just be discerned. (Great Western Trust)

Against the background of Senghenydd Colliery's chimneys, auto pannier tank No 6402 at the head of two elderly trailers stands in the station on arrival from Cardiff (Queen Street). Terminating in the Aber Valley, the Senghenydd branch from Caerphilly was built by the Rhymney Railway and closed to passengers on 15 June 1964. A gas explosion at the colliery in 1913 claimed the lives of 439 miners, making it Britain's worst mining disaster. The colliery closed in 1988. (R.W. Jones/Online Transport Archive)

An auto train hauled by pannier tank No 6438 is pictured arriving at Nantgarw on the former Pontypridd, Caerphilly and Newport Railway. Originally built for coal traffic, the line was developed for passenger services by the introduction of steam railmotors in 1904 and the provision of ground level halts such as Nantgarw. There was also another Nantgarw Halt on the Cardiff Railway designated Nantgarw Low Level in 1924 while the one shown here became Nantgarw Upper Level. However, this appellation became unnecessary when the Low Level halt closed in 1931. (R.W. Jones/Online Transport Archive)

The next station northwards from Nantgarw was Groeswen where, in this view, a mother and child wait to climb aboard. With no raised platform, shelter or fenced enclosure for protection, the boy could well be terrified as No 6402 bears down upon him at such close quarters. He and his mother are standing beside the remains of the signal box and on the site of a former siding. Groeswen and Nantgarw (above) closed when passenger services were withdrawn on 17 September 1956. (R.W. Jones/Online Transport Archive)

Trelewis Halt was on the east to west Taff Vale Extension line, located between Quakers Yard and Nelson & Llancaich. In addition to local services, trains on the Neath to Pontypool route passed through as depicted in this picture of large prairie tank No 4169 from Neath depot. The Halt opened in 1934 and closed when local passenger services were withdrawn on 15 June 1964. The Halt has vanished, but a single line passes through the site. (Great Western Trust)

The Taff Vale Extension line was built by the Newport, Abergavenny and Hereford Railway primarily for coal traffic and another station on the line was Pontypool (Clarence Street) where 0-6-2 tank No 5649 is pictured in this view. This locomotive was shedded at Aberdare for most of its post-war service life until withdrawal in April 1963. The station site has since been obliterated by the A472 dual carriageway. (Great Western Trust)

An unidentified Pannier tank stands at Maesycwmmer with a southbound train. This station on the former Brecon & Merthyr Railway closed with the other stations on this line on 31 December 1962. In the background is Hengoed Viaduct which carried the Taff Vale Extension of the Newport, Abergavenny & Hereford Railway over the Rhymney River. This line closed on 15 June 1964 and the viaduct, which is Grade II* Listed, is now a cycle route. (Great Western Trust)

We now move to the Newport-Pontypool (Crane Street)-Blaenavon line where No 9482, a Hawksworth pannier tank from Ebbw Junction, Newport, shed (86A), is operating a service calling at Cwmffrwd Halt. This locomotive was built for BR by Robert Stephenson & Hawthorn Ltd and entered service in September 1952. It was withdrawn in November 1963 and scrapped after a particularly short service life of just eleven years. (Great Western Trust)

An elderly non-auto pannier tank dating from 1929 in the 57xx number series attracts the attention of a small child as it stops at Cwmavon (Monmouth), between Cwmffrwd Halt and Blaenavon Lower Level. This line closed to passengers on 30 April 1962. The locomotive was allocated to Pontypool Road depot (86G) and could be No 5750, 5756 or 5759 (the final digit is not visible in this or the following picture). All three were withdrawn in the period 1960-1. (Great Western Trust)

The same train seen at Cwmavon has now arrived at Blaenavon Low Level. The GWR and the LNWR were rivals for the lucrative coal traffic from the pits to the docks with the result that the LNWR also built a line from Newport to Blaenavon. Their station was known as Blaenavon High Level which closed in 1941. It has since been recreated by the heritage Pontypool & Blaenavon Railway. (Great Western Trust)

Now we come to some stations which are still open, although their appearance has completely changed. This is Heath Halt Low Level on the former Cardiff Railway line from Cardiff Central to Coryton. This branch has since been singled but there are proposals to make it double track again and electrify it. This view depicts auto-fitted small prairie No 4580 propelling its train back to Cardiff. (R.W. Jones/Online Transport Archive)

The next station west of Heath Halt is Rhiwbina where No 4580 from Cardiff (Cathays) depot (88A) is seen heading for Coryton. The locomotive was withdrawn in June 1958. Coryton became the terminus for passenger trains when the line was cut back from Rhydyfelin in 1931 although freight operation on the old route continued until 1951. The Taff Vale Railway had blocked a proposed extension beyond Rhydyfelin into Treforest. (R.W. Jones/Online Transport Archive)

Another surviving station is Radyr, also on the outskirts of Cardiff, which was opened by the Taff Vale Railway. Trains from this station currently reach many destinations and there are even services to Coryton with talk of a direct loop line. This snowy scene features ex-Rhymney Railway class A 0-6-2 tank No 55 on a mineral train. A powerful locomotive, it was built in 1910, reboilered by the GWR in 1929 and withdrawn in February 1953. (R.W. Jones/Online Transport Archive)

Taffs Well station on the extreme left of this picture is another one that is still open and stands between Radyr and Treforest on the former Taff Vale Railway line from Cardiff to Merthyr. On the station platform is Walnut Tree Junction signal box which was closed in 1997 and dismantled for heritage railway use. Descending 'Big Hill' on the former Rhymney Railway Penhros branch is a coal train from the Rhymney Valley hauled by a 56xx 0-6-2 tank. This mineral line closed in 1982. (R.W. Jones/Online Transport Archive)

Ex-Taff Vale Railway class A 0-6-2 tank No 343 brings a train of empty mineral wagons under Walnut Tree viaduct as it heads towards the junction at Taffs Well. No 343 was built by Hawthorn Leslie in 1914 and was withdrawn in October 1955. The viaduct carried the Barry Railway line from Trehafod to Barry Docks and was built in 1901. The line closed to passengers on 22 July 1963 and to freight on 14 December 1967. Demolition of the viaduct started in 1969 but two brick buttresses survive. (R.W. Jones/Online Transport Archive)

Ex-Rhymney Railway R class 0-6-2 No 43 shunts at Taffs Well. The number of tracks at this point has now been reduced to two. The locomotive, seen here with a Cardiff (Cathays)/Radyr shedcode (88A), was built by Beyer Peacock in 1921 and withdrawn in February 1957. On the extreme right is part of Walnut Tree viaduct. (R.W. Jones/Online Transport Archive)

Llantrisant, on the Cardiff-Swansea mainline, was a busy junction with its own engine shed. The station closed on 2 November 1964, only to be reopened as Pontyclun in 1992, but with just two tracks and bus shelters on the platforms. Large prairie tank No 3100 storms down the main line while 0-4-2 tank No 1470 waits in the bay with an Ely Valley auto train. No 3100 was numbered 3173 when built as a member of the 3150 class in 1907 and was rebuilt in 1938, creating the 3100 class. It was withdrawn in May 1957. (R.W. Jones/Online Transport Archive)

A pair of unusual carriages headed by a 56XX 0-6-2 tank stand at Llantrisant. These were originally Taff Vale Railway articulated steam railmotors (the passenger section being attached to the cab of a steam locomotive). They were built in 1903 and subsequently converted into auto trailers. In the background on the extreme left is the combined coaling stage/water tank at the engine shed. When the shed closed in October 1964 there were still fourteen locomotives allocated there. (R.W. Jones/Online Transport Archive)

Llantrisant was also the starting point of a branch to Aberthaw and the main intermediate station was Cowbridge which is pictured here prior to closure to passengers on 24 November 1951. Freight services continued until 1 February 1965. The station site is now a housing estate. The crew pose beside auto-fitted pannier tank No 6426 which is attached to an early former steam railmotor with vertical matchboard sides. (R.W. Jones/Online Transport Archive)

0-4-2 tank No 1470 enters Penygraig on the former Ely Valley Railway with a single auto trailer. The sign on the station fence in the centre of the picture states 'Timber Platform, Out of Use.' The branch continued beyond Penygraig to Blaen-Clydach for mineral traffic. Passenger services to Penygraig were withdrawn on 9 June 1958. Later that year No 1471 was transferred to Exeter where it worked the branches in the Tiverton area until withdrawal in October 1963. (R.W. Jones/Online Transport Archive)

A head is visible through the aperture cut into the back of the end carriage of this miners' train at Glyncorrwg, the opening enabling the guard to watch the road ahead when the train was being propelled up the rising gradient between Glyncorrwg and North Rhondda Halt. This line was part of the South Wales Mineral Railway built for the transportation of coal from the Afan Valley to Briton Ferry. Glyncorrwg station closed to normal passenger services in 1930 but miners' trains continued until 2 November 1964. (R.W. Jones/Online Transport Archive)

Some miners trudge up to North Rhondda Halt to travel to Glyncorrwg in the last four-wheeled passenger carriages operated by BR. These trains were needed because there was no road access to North Rhondda colliery which, incidentally, was something of a misnomer because it was not located in the Rhondda valley but in the Corrwg valley. The halt, which closed in March 1963, is being visited here by pannier tank No 9634 from Duffryn Yard (Port Talbot) depot, coded 87B. (R.W. Jones/Online Transport Archive)

Returning to the former Brecon & Merthyr Railway and moving further northwards from Maesycwmmer (page 66). the next station was Fleur-de-lis, near Caerphilly, with pannier tank No 3767 seen at the platform. This station opened in 1926 and closed on 31 December 1962. It was named after the local village which received its French name, meaning Lily Flower, following an influx of Huguenot refugees in the seventeenth century escaping persecution who wanted to be reminded of their homeland. (Great Western Trust)

An elderly pannier tank, No 7787 from 1930, pulls into Aberbargoed station on the ex-Brecon & Merthyr Railway Rhymney branch from Newport. Aberbargoed Junction, to the south of Aberbargoed and north of Fleur-de-lis, was the point at which the Rhymney branch split off from the line to Brecon. Since the closure of Aberbargoed station on 31 December 1962, the railway platforms and buildings, along with the hotel behind, have been demolished and the site is now woodland. (Great Western Trust)

The next station northwards from Aberbargoed on the ex- Brecon & Merthyr Rhymney branch was Cwmsyfiog & Brithdir (later just Cwmsyfiog). This station closed to normal passenger services in 1937 and was renamed Cwmsyfiog Colliery Halt to serve miners. At the same time a new halt was opened for scheduled passenger trains, Cwmsyfiog Halt, and this is the location of the train seen here, hauled by pannier tank No 4671. Both halts closed on 31 December 1962. (Great Western Trust)

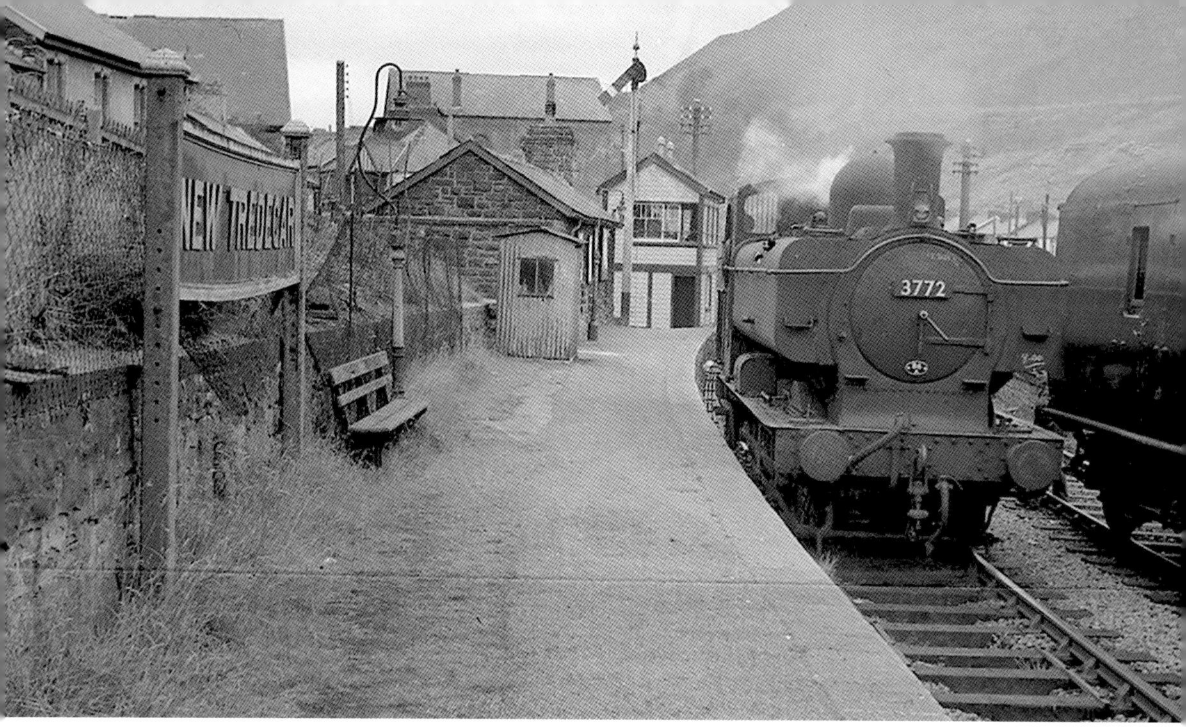

We end this visit to the Rhymney branch of the former Brecon & Merthyr Railway at New Tredegar, four stations south of the Rhymney terminus. This view shows pannier tank No 3772 running round its train. When New Tredegar was opened by the Rumney Railway prior to acquisition by the Brecon & Merthyr Railway it went by the charming name of White Rose. It received the name of New Tredegar in 1924. (Great Western Trust)

The driver of pannier tank No 3714 displays his courage and athleticism as he places the lamp on the upper bunker bracket at New Tredegar for the return journey. The fireman holds the vacuum pipe on which the driver's right leg is supported and presumably stands ready to catch him if he falls. The driver's left leg is precariously balanced on a lower lamp bracket. The locomotive was allocated to Newport (Ebbw Junction). (R.W. Jones/Online Transport Archive)

Another valley branch was the one from Newport to Nantyglo/Ebbw Vale, south of the bifurcation at Aberbeeg, which was built by the Monmouthshire Railway and Canal Company and known as their Western Valley line. One of the stations at the southern end was Crosskeys between Risca and Chapel Bridge, seen here being visited by pannier tank No 4652. The station closed on 30 April 1962 and reopened on a different site on 7 June 2008 as an intermediate station on Transport for Wales' Ebbw Valley Railway. (Great Western Trust)

A 42XX 2-8-0 tank hauls a long freight train past Celynen South Halt between Abercarn and Newbridge on the former Monmouthshire Railway and Canal Company's Western Valley line. The Halt, which opened in 1933 and closed on 30 April 1962, has not been reopened on the revived Ebbw Valley Railway. The colliery started production in 1876 and closed in 1985. The Coed Celynen housing estate now occupies the site. (Great Western Trust)

A 'Swindonised' former Taff Vale Railway 0-6-2 tank stands at Maerdy station, with another one behind. Maerdy was the terminus of the branch from Porth which closed to passengers on 15 June 1964. The tracks on the left led to Maerdy colliery which closed in 1990, making it the last pit in the Rhondda valley. The signalman appears to be looking at the cat being displayed in the cab of the engine by one of the crew. (R.W. Jones/Online Transport Archive)

Small prairie tank No 5544 enters Newbridge, Caerphilly, located between Abercarn and Crumlin Low Level on the former Monmouthshire Railway and Canal Company line. A new station was built for the resurrection of the Cardiff-Ebbw Vale line and this opened on 6 February 2008. When this photograph was taken No 5544, which was built in 1928, was allocated to Aberbeeg depot where it was based from 1955 to 1960. It was withdrawn in September 1962 and scrapped. (Great Western Trust)

Entering the 1960s Penrhiwceiber boasted two railway stations on separate lines, the former Taff Vale Railway branch to Aberdare with trains calling at Penrhiwceiber Low Level station and the one featured in this view. This was the High Level station on the former Vale of Neath Railway's Neath to Pontypool Road line via Mountain Ash and Quakers Yard. This photograph depicts 0-6-2 tank No 6651 which was based at Aberdare throughout the 1950s until withdrawal in February 1963. (Great Western Trust)

Proceeding north west along the former Vale of Neath Railway from Penrhiwceiber we reach Gelly Tarw Junction, where that Railway's branch to Merthyr split from the line to Neath. Beyond the junction and immediately before Hirwaun (Hirwain before September 1928) was Llwydcoed where an auto train with No 6433 in charge is seen on a Hirwaun-Merthyr service. Closure to passengers came on 31 December 1962. See also page 118. (Great Western Trust)

Several railway companies were keen to reach Dowlais, adjacent to Merthyr, to access the area's mineral traffic. This picture depicts Dowlais Cae Harris station which was the terminus of the Rhymney Railway's branch from Treharris and closed on 15 June 1964. The terminus also had a substantial locomotive sub-shed. The clerestory-roofed carriages superseded the four-wheelers on miners' trains. By December 1951 only eleven of the latter remained. (R.W. Jones/Online Transport Archive)

Heading northwards along the Neath & Brecon Railway from Neath Riverside we come to Penscynor Halt which was immediately south of Cilfrew at the Neath end of the line. Indeed, it was one of eight stations officially termed 'halts' between Neath and Onllyn. Penscynor Halt, seen here with pannier tank No 4621 passing through with a freight, opened in 1929 and closed on 15 October 1962. (Great Western Trust)

This is Onllyn station in the Upper Dulais Valley, immediately south of Colbren Junction, on the former Neath & Brecon Railway, which opened in 1867 and closed on 15 October 1962. A nearby coal-washing plant ensured the line's consequent survival for freight traffic to Newport but this has now closed, along with a nearby open-cast mine, and both sites are due to be used for a new train testing facility. (Great Western Trust)

In July 1962, my school's Combined Cadet Force Annual Camp took place at Sennybridge and we travelled there to the station depicted here by train via Hereford, Three Cocks Junction (which generated some schoolboy sniggers!) and Brecon. The impending closure of the route would have rendered the journey west of Hereford impossible some two and a half months later. Here we see pannier tank No 3687 from Neath (Court Sart) depot. Sennybridge was added to the station's name in 1913. (Great Western Trust)

Heading towards Talyllyn Junction from the south on the former Brecon & Merthyr Railway's line from Pontsticill Junction brings us to Torpantau where pannier tank No 9665 from Hereford depot (85C) is depicted here hauling an ammonia train from Swansea to the north of England. Torpantau is now the northern terminus of the narrow gauge Brecon Mountain Railway from Pant although the present station which opened on 1 April 2014 is on an adjacent site across the road from the original one. (Great Western Trust)

Talyllyn Junction was triangular in layout, where the Brecon & Merthyr Railway met the Mid-Wales Railway, both heading for Brecon. The junction closed to passengers on 31 December 1962 and to freight on 4 May 1964. The original Brecon & Merthyr Railway main station building is now a private residence. This view depicts 2251 class 0-6-0 No 2218 on a southbound service to Newport having just emerged from Talyllyn tunnel. (Great Western Trust)

The Mid-Wales Railway was acquired by the Cambrian Railway in 1904 and this is one of the latter's 0-6-0 tender engines, No 887, which was built by Robert Stephenson & Hawthorn in 1903 and withdrawn in November 1952. The train is heading for Talgarth, Three Cocks Junction and Builth Wells. The lines curving to the right are those of the Brecon & Merthyr Railway to Torpantau, Pontsticill Junction and Merthyr. (R.W. Jones/Online Transport Archive)

Immediately south of Three Cocks Junction on the Mid-Wales/Cambrian line was Talgarth station seen here as 2251 class 0-6-0 No 2218 makes its way to Trefeinon and Talyllyn Junction. Closure to passengers occurred on 31 December 1962 and the trackbed is now the A479 road. However, although the water tower, signal box and shelter have vanished all the station buildings on the left survive as residential accommodation and protected from the road by a stone wall. (Great Western Trust)

Here is a distinctive running-in board which pre-dates the addition of the suffix 'Junction' to the station name. The renaming may have been due to public sensitivities, particularly since the station was apparently nicknamed Lucky Man Junction. It was opened by the Mid-Wales Railway and became part of the Cambrian Railway but it also served the Hereford, Hay and Brecon Railway which was subsequently absorbed by the Midland Railway. (Great Western Trust)

Great Western Branch Line Gallery • 85

We end this tour of the Central Wales lines at Builth Wells (Low Level). When the station was opened by the Mid-Wales Railway in 1864 it was named Llechryd and received its later name in 1889. Until it closed to passengers on 31 December 1962 it served as an interchange with the High Level station from which this photograph was taken. This latter station was built by the Central Wales Extension Railway (later the LNWR) and is currently a request stop on the Heart of Wales line. The former Low Level station buildings have been converted into a pub called the Cambrian Arms. This picture depicts Ivatt 2-6-0 No 46509 on a northbound train heading towards Llanidloes and Moat Lane Junction. (R.W. Jones/Online Transport Archive)

Moving westwards along the South Wales coast from Neath and Swansea brings us to Llanelly. Here the Llanelly Railway and Dock Company built a branch from Pontardulais to Brynamman. One of the intermediate stations was Glanamman where pannier tank No 3777 is standing with a two-coach train. Passenger services were withdrawn on 18 August 1958 and on 30 January 1965 for goods but there were coal mines and tin plate works in the Amman Valley and sporadic mineral traffic in recent years has resulted in the track remaining in situ. (Great Western Trust)

The ex-GWR terminus at Brynamman, seen here hosting a railtour on 2 July 1955, received the suffix 'west' in 1950 to distinguish it from the ex-Midland Railway station. This became Brynamman East at the same time but closed to passengers on 25 September 1950, rendering the suffixes rather pointless. In the platform stands an ex-LMS push and pull driving car (M24401) hauled by LMS Jinty No 47480, an incongruous combination for this BR(W) branch. (R.W. Jones/Online Transport Archive)

Something of a problem seems to have occurred at Horeb on the Llanelly and Mynydd Mawr Railway's mineral branch from Llanelly to Cross Hands. Prior to 1950 when some realignment of track took place due to expansion of the Cynheidre colliery the line had very sharp curves, but this is unlikely to be the cause of the derailment depicted here particularly since the picture is believed to have been taken around 1958. No passenger trains ever operated on this line apart from workmen's services. The branch ceased operation when the colliery closed in 1989. (R.W. Jones/Online Transport Archive)

The rescue squad has just arrived to deal with the offending mineral wagon (see previous page). The train contains a Tool Van and Riding Van from Llanelly depot. The building in the background is Horeb Welsh Baptist Chapel at Five Roads, Llanelly, built in 1868 and Grade II Listed, but currently disused. (R.W. Jones/Online Transport Archive)

Pannier tank No 1643, at the head of a long train of mineral wagons, takes water at Cynheidre. A heritage railway organisation, using the original company name but with the latterday Llanelli spelling, is based on the site of the former Cynheidre colliery and aims to reopen as much of the original branch as possible. (R.W. Jones/Online Transport Archive)

Slightly to the west of the Cross Hands mineral branch was the Burry Port and Gwendraeth Valley Railway. This carried passengers from Burry Port to Cwm Mawr until 19 September 1953. Burry Port had a sub shed linked to Llanelly (87F) which closed in February 1962 and where No 1609 was based. Behind the Neptune Hotel (now called The Neptune) visible in the background is the former GWR West Wales line. The adjacent station, Pembrey and Burry Port, remains open whereas the station seen here has been obliterated. (R.W. Jones/Online Transport Archive)

No 1609 has now arrived at Cwm Mawr and is preparing to return to Burry Port. Despite the closure to passengers in 1953 the line remained open to freight until 1996, this traffic consisting of coal trains until the collieries in the area closed down. No 1609 had a typically short life for this type of light pannier tank, entering service in November 1949 and being withdrawn in July 1962. (R.W. Jones/Online Transport Archive)

Westward beyond Burry Port on the former GWR West Wales line is Carmarthen where there was a route to Aberystwyth. The first station north of Carmarthen was Bronwydd Arms, being visited here by 4-6-0 No 7829 **Ramsbury Manor**. This line closed to passengers on 22 February 1965 and Bronwydd Arms is now the headquarters of the heritage Gwili Railway which currently operates a four mile stretch and aims to extend further. The station building depicted here was demolished but a replacement has been built. **(Great Western Trust)**

Moving further west brings us to Whitland, junction for the former Cardigan branch which was some 27 miles long and closed to passengers on 10 September 1962. The fourth station along the line was Llanfyrnach and this view shows small prairie tank No 4558 entering the platform. St Brynach church can be seen in the background. See also page 120. **(Great Western Trust)**

There is a branch to Pembroke Dock which diverges from the Fishguard line at Whitland and unlike the Cardigan branch is still open today. This is Penally, an intermediate station between Tenby and Manorbier, and pictured here as a large prairie tank arrives from Pembroke Dock. Penally station closed on 15 June 1964 and was permanently reopened on 28 February 1972. However, the reasonably substantial platform building has given way to a basic passenger shelter. (Great Western Trust)

Pannier tank No 4677 enters Wolfs Castle for Treffgarne Rocks on its way to Fishguard and Goodwick station. The locomotive was shedded at Goodwick between November 1954 and October 1962. Wolfs Castle was located on the Carmarthen-Fishguard line and was closed on 6 April 1964. The track at this point has now been singled and centralised, thereby making any future use of the one surviving platform impracticable. (Great Western Trust)

Passenger services on the ex-Cambrian Railway narrow-gauge Welshpool & Llanfair Light Railway ceased on 9 February 1931 but freight continued under the auspices of BR(W) until 3 November 1956. There were Exchange Sidings located at Welshpool where No 822 **The Earl** is pictured. In the background is the standard gauge station located on the Shrewsbury to Newtown route. This building has since been converted for retail use and replaced by one on the opposite side of the Welshpool by-pass (A483) following track realignment. See also pages 121 & 122. (John Scott-Morgan collection)

Another Welsh narrow gauge railway acquired by the GWR from the Cambrian Railway was the Vale of Rheidol Light Railway which operated a 12-mile route from Aberystwyth to Devil's Bridge. The three GWR-built locomotives dating from 1922-3 were BR's last operating steam locomotives until the line was privatised in 1989, with no break in service. This view taken in GWR days depicts No 7 taking water at Aberffrwd before undertaking the 1 in 50 climb to Devil's Bridge. See also page 122. (**Author's collection**)

The Aberystwyth-Carmarthen line closed in two stages. Caradog Falls, seen here being visited by 7829 *Ramsbury Manor* (also depicted on page 90 at the lower end of the line) was a halt opened in 1932 and located at the upper end between Strata Florida and Trawscoed. Severe flooding north of Strata Florida caused the route, including this halt, to close prematurely on 14 December 1964. The line south of Strata Florida closed on schedule on 22 February 1965. (Great Western Trust)

Barmouth, on the Cambrian Coast line, had a bay platform south of the main station and level crossing (visible on the left) which was used for trains to Dolgelley, the destination of the auto train depicted here. The line, which continued to Ruabon, closed on 18 January 1965. The locomotive, No 1430, is a George Armstrong 517 class 0-4-2, forerunner of the Collett 48XX/14XX auto-fitted 0-4-2 tanks. The auto trailer in this picture, Collett No 178 dating from 1930, is preserved and based at the Severn Valley Railway. (Great Western Trust)

Eastward from Dolgelley was Bala Junction where a branch headed off to Blaenau Festiniog. The first station on the line was Bala where this picture was taken. This was the so-called Bala New station, replacing the original one on the Barmouth-Ruabon line in 1882. The locomotive is No 1780 which belonged to the 655 class of saddletanks. It was built in 1893 and fitted with pannier tanks in 1921. Withdrawal and scrapping occurred in 1948 after 55 years of service. (Great Western Trust)

Further along the branch to Blaenau Festiniog was Festiniog station which closed to passengers on 4 January 1960. Freight services were withdrawn on 28 January 1961 but the upper end of the line as far as Trawsfynydd nuclear power station reopened on 10 April 1964 before finally closing on 17 October 1998. This section of line is currently mothballed. The vehicle in this view is a railway engineering personnel carrier, Wickham trolley No B182W. (Great Western Trust)

Three companies used to operate into Blaenau Festiniog at the time this picture was taken: the LNWR from Llandudno, the narrow gauge Festiniog Railway from Portmadoc and the GWR from Bala. This view depicts a pannier tank on arrival at the GWR terminus where the Festiniog Railway had an interchange platform. This closed on 18 September 1939 and the BR(W) station closed to passengers on 4 January 1960 and to freight on 28 January 1961. (Great Western Trust)

A mixed train headed by pannier tank No 7414 stands at Blaenau Ffestiniog Central station (its official name since 18 June 1951). With the opening of the Trawsfynydd nuclear power station and the abandonment of the lower part of the line due to the construction of a reservoir the ex-LNWR line was extended to the BR(W) station in 1964 and this is now the site of the joint National Rail/Ffestiniog Railway station which was officially opened in 1983. (R.W. Jones/Online Transport Archive)

This early photograph of the GWR's Blaenau Festiniog station shows the narrow gauge Festiniog Railway platform face on the left. The new exchange station built on the site now has the Festiniog Railway on the right hand side. A pannier tank-hauled train stands in the platform outside the main station building. In the centre background is the Queens Hotel at 1 High Street. This is still extant but there has been a dispute over the name since it was renamed the Gwesty Ty Gorsaf Hotel in 2012. (Great Western Trust)

There were transhipment sidings at Blaenau Festiniog for the carriage of slate from the mines which was brought to the GWR station by the Festiniog Railway. This photograph shows the narrow/standard gauge crossover enabling the Festiniog Railway's slate wagons to reach the sidings beyond the Goods Shed visible in the distance. This interchange traffic ceased in 1945 as demand for slates had been decreasing and the Festiniog Railway in its pre-preservation existence closed in 1946. (R.W. Jones/Online Transport Archive)

In this view a number of empty Festiniog Railway slate wagons stand atop a GWR flat wagon at Blaenau Festiniog's slate transfer yard. The standard gauge transporter wagons were designed for end loading and were fitted with narrow gauge tracks on the deck which could accommodate six slate wagons (three side by side as seen here). (R.W. Jones/Online Transport Archive)

This final view of Blaenau Festiniog shows the narrow gauge tracks occupied by Festiniog Railway slate wagons on either side of the GWR tracks. In the centre is a set of four-wheeled carriages. The nearest one is W81, the Oswestry Electricians Tool Van. The passenger station sits behind the suburban carriage towards the left and the Queens Hotel stands proudly in the centre background. (R.W. Jones/Online Transport Archive)

Continuing along the Barmouth-Ruabon line the station eastwards beyond Bala Junction was Llandderfel. This was close to the location of the River Dee flooding which caused the line to be closed without warning on 4 December 1964 rather than on the scheduled date of 18 January 1965. Here we see pannier tank No 4645 entering the station from Bala Junction heading for Corwen. The station buildings in this picture have all been demolished. (Great Western Trust)

We end our journey on the Barmouth-Ruabon line at Bonwm Halt which was located between Corwen and Carrog. The halt opened on 21 September 1935 and closed on 14 December 1964 when the line flooded. There is now no trace of the halt, but trains pass through the site because it is situated on the heritage Llangollen Railway which operates between Llangollen (to the west of Ruabon) and a new station at Corwen East. (Great Western Trust)

Here are two GWR absorbed engines built for Welsh railway companies. The saddletank is No 776 constructed by Hudswell Clarke in 1905 and one of 28 Barry Railway class F locomotives. It was sold to Powell Duffryn in 1933 and worked at Aberaman Colliery. It was scrapped in 1960. The side tank is No 2197, ex Burry Port and Gwendreath Valley Railway No 8 *Pioneer*, built by Hudswell Clarke in 1909 and withdrawn by BR in 1952. (R W Jones/Online Transport Archive - both)

We end the monochrome section of this gallery with two more photographs of GWR absorbed locomotives. The first features a rare example of an 0-4-0 pannier tank. This is **Dorothy**, built by Brush as a saddletank in 1903 and originally Powlesland & Mason (P&M) No 5, becoming GWR No 795 and fitted with pannier tanks in 1926. It was sold in 1929 and ended its days at the Pontardawe tinplate works north east of Swansea. Sister locomotive P&M No 6 (GWR 921) remained a saddletank and has been preserved. Finally, here is GWR/BR No 155, an ex-Cardiff Railway 0-6-2 tank built by Kitson in 1908 and withdrawn in 1953. (R.W. Jones/Online Transport Archive - both)

The open ground seen here on the east side of the Greenford to West Ealing loop between Castle Bar Park Halt and Drayton Green Halt has since been built over and a new road inserted between the railway and the distant houses in Cavendish Avenue. Viewed from Drayton Bridge Road, a 54XX pannier tank is propelling auto coach Wren towards Drayton Green Halt on its way to West Ealing and Ealing Broadway. The steam auto-trains were replaced by diesel 'bubble cars' from 25 August 1958. (Julian Thompson/Online Transport Archive)

A colourful display of billboard advertising welcomes passengers to Marlow in this view of the station's exterior while an auto train stands in the platform. The service was dieselised from 9 July 1962 and still operates between Maidenhead via Bourne End but Marlow station as seen here has been demolished after a replacement was built further back on the goods yard site. (Great Western Trust)

The station after Bourne End travelling towards High Wycombe was Wooburn Green which possessed a relatively active goods yard and boasted a small signal box on the platform. Along with the station it remained gas lit to the end as evidenced by this picture of the signalman on duty. (Author)

Princes Risborough's third branch line was the one to Watlington which terminated near Pyrton, some distance from Watlington. Passenger services were withdrawn on 1 July 1957, but some remnants of the terminus remain today within a farm in Station Road, a narrow lane off the B 4009. The most visible is the corrugated iron carriage shed on the left of the picture. This view was taken when a railtour hauled by 0-4-2 tank No 1473 visited the Watlington branch on 3 April 1960. (Charles Firminger/ Online Transport Archive)

Diesel single unit 'bubble cars' such as this one operated Abingdon branch services from 1959, replacing the 14XX auto trains. The terminus station building behind the diesel dated from 1909 as the original one built for the opening of the line in 1856 had been seriously damaged in a railway accident. Following the withdrawal of passenger trains, freight services, mainly the transportation of new MG cars, continued until final closure of the branch in June 1984. (Great Western Trust)

A mixed train from Fairford arrives at the resited Witney station. Unusually, the locomotive is running bunker first. Fairford was a rare case of a branch line having a turntable and engines departing on passenger trains from Fairford were normally turned, thereby running in both directions smokebox first. (Great Western Trust)

Towards the end of the Lambourn Valley line was Great Shefford where this picture of 2251 class 0-6-0 No 2221 was taken. This part of the branch was closed completely on 4 January 1960 but the section at the Newbury end remained open for freight until 1972. (Great Western Trust)

Today, hardly anything has changed in this picture apart from the freight train hauled by pannier tank No 3632. Although the station has been called Avoncliff since 1969, the platforms still feature the old Avoncliff Halt running-in boards. Old style GWR benches are in place and the wooden shelters appear unchanged. Opened in 1906, it is situated in Wiltshire between Freshford and Bradford-on-Avon on the present Heart of Wessex Line. (Great Western Trust)

The GWR extended south from Yeovil to reach the Dorset coast at Weymouth and Bridport, the junction for each route being at Maiden Newton on today's Heart of Wessex line. Until 1987 boat trains would terminate at Weymouth Quay and between 1934 and 1962 these were normally hauled along the branch by one of the six-strong 1366 class of outside-cylindered pannier tanks such as the example pictured, No 1368. The last train to use the branch was a railtour in 1999. (Geoff Smith/Online Transport Archive)

The Maiden Newton-Bridport branch closed on 5 May 1975 and was latterly operated by a single car DMU. However, when steam haulage was replaced from 15 June 1959 three-car units were initially used, coinciding with the closure of the engine shed visible on the right. This view at Bridport dates from 10 April 1960. The branch originally continued to West Bay in the vain hope that a resort might be developed there but the extension closed to passengers in 1930 and to goods in 1962. (Charles Firminger/Online Transport Archive)

Latterly, the Taunton-Barnstaple line was single track beyond the first intermediate station on the branch (Milverton) apart from passing loops installed at various stations. The most important intermediate station was Dulverton, the junction for the Exe Valley line (see page 18). This view from August 1963 depicts No 7304 arriving at Swimbridge, the final station before Barnstaple, and now obliterated by the North Devon Link Road. **(Great Western Trust)**

Services on the 12-mile long GW Chard branch started at Taunton where pannier tank No 3787 was photographed in August 1962, a few weeks before the last day of passenger services on 8 September. The Hawksworth coach in chocolate and cream livery brightens the scene. (Author)

One of the intermediate stations on the Chard branch was Hatch, serving the village of Hatch Beaumont. The station building is Grade II Listed and is currently part of the Weavo Company's complex, along with the goods shed, hidden behind the station building in this view. Hatch tunnel, visible in the background, is now boarded up. Pannier tank No 3736 heads the train. (Great Western Trust)

One can still stand under this roof that once covered the GWR's Chard Central station and admire its intricate widow apertures and cast iron supports, but you would be inside the Original Factory Shop in Great Western Road, Chard, Somerset, a Grade II Listed building. This photograph taken on 10 February 1962 depicts pannier tank No 9608 in the bay platform with a train from Taunton while small prairie tank No 5554 arrives from Chard Junction. (Les Folkard/Online Transport Archive)

Two Exe Valley trains pass at Bampton station in May 1963. On the left is non-auto fitted pannier tank No 3659 and on the right is 0-4-2 tank No 1466 which was bought by the 48XX Preservation Society (now the Great Western Society) in April 1964 for £750. The Exe Valley line closed on 7 October 1963 and there is now no trace of the railway and its buildings at Bampton. (Great Western Trust)

0-4-2 tank No 1466 prepares to reverse from Moretonhampstead to Newton Abbot on 21 February 1959, one week before the last day of passenger services. Behind the auto coach is the goods shed and in the distance on the right is the engine shed and water tower. Both the goods shed and engine shed have been used latterly by a haulage company but there are plans to clear the site for a housing development. (Les Folkard/Online Transport Archive)

The so-called 'Primrose Line' from Brent to Kingsbridge closed on 16 September 1963. This view dates from 1961 just before DMUs took over, with small prairie tank No 4561 (since preserved) setting off for Brent. The branch was some 12 miles long with three intermediate stations, one of which is featured on the front cover. Plans to extend the line beyond Kingsbridge to Salcombe never materialised. (Les Folkard/Online Transport Archive)

This picture depicts a freight train in a heavily wooded section of the Launceston branch near Plym Bridge Platform in 1962 hauled by a clean 57XX pannier tank with later cab design. (Les Folkard/Online Transport Archive)

The first station on the Launceston branch was Marsh Mills, seen here with a train bound for Plymouth headed by small prairie tank No 4570 in July 1962. The heritage Plym Valley Railway has since reopened a 1.5 mile stretch from Marsh Mills (at the approximate location of the original station) to the reconstructed Plym Bridge Platform. (Les Folkard/Online Transport Archive)

The Fowey branch had one intermediate station, Golant, seen here with No 1419 arriving from Lostwithiel. The branch closed to passengers on 4 January 1965 but remains open for the transportation of china clay to the jetties at Fowey Carne Point. Golant station, located beside a stretch of water, has been replaced by a small car park. (Great Western Trust)

This pannier tank is not travelling on a Swiss mountain railway but hauling a brake van tour of the freight-only Goonbarrow branch on 22 April 1961. The train is heading for the 'Cornish Alps' which consisted of excavated china clay. This was another mineral line accessed from the Par-Newquay branch. Never having a passenger service, it was located just east of Bugle in Cornwall and was purchased by the GWR in 1896. The locomotive is lightweight pannier tank No 1626, one of two shedded at St Blazey for these workings serving several china clay kilns. From October 1964 the branch was worked as a long siding which became increasingly truncated, and all that remains now is a short stub at Goonbarrow Junction. No 1626 entered service in August 1950 and had a short service life, being scrapped in August 1963. (Les Folkard/Online Transport Archive)

This diesel railbus was photographed on a murky day at Cirencester Town station on 22 February 1964 as it prepares to operate the 10.32 am service to Kemble. The unusual station building dates from the opening of the branch in 1841 and is Grade II Listed. It was designed by Brunel. (Charles Firminger/Online Transport Archive)

The eastern section of the Banbury-Cheltenham route had several intermediate stations including Stow-on-the-Wold. Viewed from the A424 road bridge, large prairie tank No 4142 pulls out of this station on its way from Cheltenham to Kingham in May 1962. The station closed on 15 October 1962 and has since been converted for residential use although it is not visible from the public road. Kingham station remains open, being on the Cotswold Line running between Oxford, Worcester and Hereford. (Great Western Trust)

Although this is the main line between Gloucester and Swindon the stopping services introduced in 1903 which pioneered the use of steam railmotors certainly followed branch line practice with the use of auto trains stopping at local stations and unmanned halts. This photograph of 0-4-2 tank No 1458 at Cashes Green Halt was taken in October 1964 during the final month of services. This halt, located between Stonehouse (Burdett Road) and Stroud, was opened as late as 22 January 1930 to serve a new housing estate. (Great Western Trust)

The Golden Valley between Stroud and Chalford in Gloucestershire was apparently so named because of the monetary wealth generated by the local wool trade rather than the scenic beauty of the area. However, the latter interpretation is apt for this photograph of auto–fitted pannier tank No 6412 taken on the last day of passenger services between Gloucester and Chalford, 31 October 1964. Ham Mill Halt, between Stroud and Brimscombe, opened when services began in 1903 with the intention of attracting passengers away from local bus services and to counteract a possible electric tramway. (Author)

We are now moving northwards from Gloucestershire to Herefordshire for this view of the so-called Daffodil Line from Ledbury to Gloucester. Ledbury's main station remains open and is situated on the Worcester-Hereford line but the town's second station, Ledbury Town Halt, closed to passengers on 13 July 1959 when services from Gloucester were withdrawn. Here is GWR diesel railcar No W19 standing at the Halt. (Great Western Trust)

This is Bewdley station on 19 September 1965 when it was visited by a railtour hauled by two privately preserved locomotives, small prairie tank No 4555 and 0-4-2 tank No 1420. They hauled the Worcester (Shrub Hill) circular leg of the tour via Hartlebury, Bewdley, Kidderminster and Wolverhampton (Low Level). Passenger services to Bewdley were withdrawn on 6 January 1970 and resumed in 1974 under the auspices of the heritage Severn Valley Railway. (Author)

One of the lines referred to on page 49 which radiated from Bewdley went to Kidderminster and Stourbridge Junction. Kidderminster was also reached from Worcester via Droitwich. The line then continued northwards to Stourbridge Junction where large prairie tank No 4140 was photographed and where it was allocated (shed code 84F) from 1958 until withdrawal in 1963. This station remains open and services run to Kidderminster/Worcester, Stourbridge Town and Birmingham via Old Hill. (Great Western Trust)

The line from Stourbridge Junction to Wolverhampton closed to passengers on 30 July 1962 and Brettell Lane, the first station north of Stourbridge Junction, has disappeared without trace. In this photograph a local train is heading for Stourbridge Junction hauled by a large prairie tank in July 1962, the last month of passenger services. Pressure is mounting for these services to be restored as this part of the line as far as Dudley is still open for freight. (Great Western Trust)

North of Bassaleg on the Brecon & Merthyr Railway was Machen where a branch to Caerphilly split from the line to Brecon and branch to Rhymney. Machen station was closed to passengers on 31 December 1962 (and to freight on 16 July 1964) and is pictured here on 7 May 1960 on the occasion of the South Monmouthshire Rail Tour organised by the Railway & Canal Historical Society. Auto-fitted pannier tank No 6426 is 'sandwiched' because propelling was officially limited to no more than two trailers and therefore, in this scene, the third one is being pulled while the other two are being pushed. (Charles Firminger/Online Transport Archive)

On 4 November 1961 non-auto fitted pannier tank No 9631 brings a Collett auto trailer into Merthyr, this combination having formed the 10.10am service from Hirwaun. The train is passing auto-fitted pannier tank No 6433 taking water. When this photograph was taken Merthyr (High Street) station possessed four platforms and at one time had a train shed roof. The station is still open but has been reduced to a single platform and retailers occupy the remainder of the former station site. The station is now called Merthyr Tydfil. (Charles Firminger/Online Transport Archive)

Great Western Branch Line Gallery • 119

This is Cefn-Coed station on the former Brecon & Merthyr Railway and the train, headed once more by auto-fitted pannier tank No 6433, is the 9.28am northbound service from Merthyr to Pontsticill Junction, photographed on 4 November 1961. Cefn-Coed station closed to passengers on 13 November 1961 and to goods on 4 May 1964. It has since been demolished but the 15-arch viaduct over which the train has just passed before entering the station survives. It is Grade II Listed and is now part of the Taff Trail footpath and cycleway. Until 1920, Cefn-Coed station was simply called Cefn. (Charles Firminger/Online Transport Archive)

There were two separate stations at Dowlais Top. One served the former LNWR line from Merthyr to Abergavenny while the one shown here is the ex- Brecon & Merthyr Railway station on the line heading north to Pant, Torpantau and Brecon. The station closed on 31 December 1962. Pannier tank No 9616 from Newport (Ebbw Junction) shed is working a Brecon-Newport service. (Marcus Eavis/Online Transport Archive)

Seen on the Cardigan branch is small prairie tank, No 4557, standing at Crymmych Arms, named after a pub. That is still there, just round the corner from Station Road, but has adopted the later spelling with only one letter m. Rather unusually, the Down platform evident here had its awning attached to the goods shed. The main station building and stationmaster's house were on the Up platform, here obscured by trees. These buildings still exist, along with the goods shed. (Great Western Trust)

Three abortive attempts were made in the nineteenth century to build a railway between Llanfair Caereinion and Welshpool in Wales, primarily to facilitate the movement of supplies to and from the farming community. These schemes failed due to the inability to raise sufficient capital. However, the Light Railways Act of 1896 reduced the costs of creating rural railways, as well as simplifying legal requirements, and the railway, using a narrow gauge of 2ft 6ins, was built at the start of the twentieth century, with passenger services commencing on 4 April 1903. Two Beyer Peacock 0-6-0 tank engines were constructed for the line in the previous year, which were later named after the Earl of Powis and his wife, the Countess, in recognition of their support. The line was operated by the Cambrian Railway which also owned the standard gauge route through Welshpool. The Cambrian was amalgamated in 1922 with the GWR which subsequently 'Great Westernised' the locomotives and renumbered them 822 and 823. This view depicts the former No 2, Countess, shunting in the goods yard at Welshpool. (John McCann/Online Transport Archive)

Upon closure of the Welshpool & Llanfair in 1956, there was immediate interest in preserving the line and BR stored the two engines in Oswestry Works for some four years until the Preservation Company was formally set up. The Company leased the line from BR in late 1962, reopening the upper end to the public in April 1963 and purchased it in March 1974. However, the town centre section had to be abandoned. Here is No 822 in Brook Street passing the entrance to Meadow View. The building and railings on the right remain in place today. (Phil Tatt/Online Transport Archive)

Interested children watch No 9 *Prince of Wales* cross Park Avenue after leaving Aberystwyth station for Devil's Bridge in the late 1950s. Vale of Rheidol trains started using the redundant Carmarthen line platforms in the main station (visible in the background) from 1968. As a result, there is no longer a level crossing at this point; the railway now runs parallel with the standard gauge line for some distance before crossing a more minor road. The three locomotives received their names in 1956. (Phil Tatt/Online Transport Archive)